THE TALL SHIPS

A SALUTE TO LIBERTY

P9-BHX-717

OP SAIL '86

The Official book of Operation Sail, 1986

Introduction by William F. Buckley, Jr.
Text by Charles Flowers

PHOTOGRAPHS BY

Joel Greenberg

Alexis Gregory, Dan Nerney,
Dan Nelken, Stanley Rosenfeld, and Frank Rohr

THE VENDOME PRESS

Photo credits © 1986

Joel Greenberg: pgs. 3, 6, 32, 38, 39, 40 *bottom*, 41, 52, 62-63, 66-67, 80, 87, 90, 91, 92–93, 96, 98–99, 101 *bottom*, 105, 108, 109, 110–111, 112, 114, 124 *bottom*, 125 *top*, 126.

Alexis Gregory: pgs. 36, 37, 42, 49, 54, 62, 70, 74–75, 81, 84, 104 *bottom*.

Dan Nelken: pgs. 94, 100, 123, 125 *bottom*, 128.

Dan Nerney: pgs. 85, 104 *top*, 115, 118–119, 127.

Frank Rohr: pgs. 40 *top*, 68, 69, 71, 83.

Stanley Rosenfeld: pgs. 9, 72, 78–79, 82, 95, 97, 101 *top*, 102, 103, 106–107, 117.

Black Star Photo Agency: Dennis Brack, 11. Tom Sobolik, 12–13. Rick Friedman, 120. Christopher Morris, 122. James Kamp, 124 *top*.

Mystic Seaport Museum: pgs. 16, 18–27.

Page 113 courtesy of The White House

Cover photograph by Joel Greenberg

Back cover photograph by Alexis Gregory

Published in the United States of America by
The Vendome Press
515 Madison Avenue
New York, New York 10022

Distributed in the United States of America by
Rizzoli International Publications, 597 Fifth Avenue, New York 10017

Designer: Deborah Michel

© 1986 The Vendome Press, New York City

Text © 1986 Charles Flowers
Introduction © 1986 William F. Buckley, Jr.

All rights reserved

Library of Congress Cataloging-in-Publication Data
The Tall Ships.

   1. Operation Sail, 1986.   2. Sailing ships.
3. Training-ships.   4. Statue of Liberty
(New York, N.Y.)—Centennial celebrations, etc.
I. Buckley, William F. (William Frank), 1925–
VK20.T34   1986   797.1'24'097474   86–19064

ISBN 0–86565–073–X
ISBN 0–86565–074–8 (pbk.)

Color separations by Colorscan Overseas Co. Pty. Ltd., Singapore

Printing by R. R. Donnelley & Sons Company, Willard, Ohio

Printed and bound in the U.S.A.

*The fiercely protective figurehead of the **Eagle** gleams proudly on the famous ship's 50th birthday. As official host of Operation Sail 1986, she led off the Parade of Sail on July 4, a jubilant progress of more than 235 notable sailing vessels from the Verrazano Bridge up the Hudson River to the George Washington Bridge and back downstream to berths in lower Manhattan and Brooklyn.*

(Special thanks to Sohei Hohri, Librarian and Curator, The New York Yacht Club, and Leslie Slocum, Librarian, Television Information Office.)

CONTENTS

Foreword

by William F. Buckley, Jr.

There was much ado ahead of the event about the Hollywoodization of Liberty Weekend, rumors of vulgarities that would have made the worst excesses of Cecil B. DeMille seem monkish by comparison. There are two competing sensibilities at play, in the field of American celebrations: the Apollonians would have us stand on a patch of bare earth, reciting the Declaration of Independence (silently; to ourselves) our accompaniment only the tolling of a lone churchyard bell, whereafter we would re-read the *Federalist Papers* and go to sleep. The Dionysians would have . . . something else: elephants, bunting, fireworks, the Blue Angels, coast-to-coast live satellite hookups, Sousaphones in excelsis, costumes borrowed from Liberace's wardrobe, a stage borrowed from Caesar's Palace in Las Vegas, lasers, the works! *Can we get Wayne Newton to parachute in for the finale singing Danke shoen?*

In the end, the Dionysians carried the day, though it was hardly all that awful. The over-vilified Hollywood producer who stage-managed the affair had put his foot down here and there, refusing for instance the kind offer of the Hawaiian group that had proposed dropping a two-ton lei of flowers by Chinook helicopter onto Miss Liberty's shoulders at the climactic moment. Sure, we could have done without the magenta-electric stage, the uniforms on the band, most of the music (I am thinking of the original compositions, not the *Star-Spangled Banner*, which is bad enough, musically), the cavalcade of Hollywood types. The critical mass of them that evening suggested that what was about to be unveiled was a gigantic Oscar, rather than Monsieur Bartholdi's refurbished masterpiece.

And yet . . . and yet, amid the glimmer, shimmer, glitz and ritz of it all were the incomparably American grace notes: the thirteen-year-old black teenager singing the national anthem, singing his heart out; the Chief Justice of the United States administering the oath of citizenship to thousands of new Americans. As he led the crowd, asking them whether they would take up arms in the defense of their new country, the camera panned toward the back, where a young Chinese boy, no more than four years old and carried on his father's shoulder, stared innocently and not-quite-comprehendingly at the proceedings in which he was playing such a iconographic part, his father holding his small hand over his heart.

It was an exaltation not so much of the New World, as of the common man. In his speech, that windy, cool night, President Reagan touched down on all the lapidary phrases—"nation of immigrants", "hope to the world for all future time", "shining city on a hill"—but he also used one that was new to me: "mother of exiles." That was, after all, what they were, those hundreds of thousands who stood gazing at her from the steerage decks, the Boat People of the American past. When the little Vietnamese girl who

had won the essay contest got up to speak of her own long journey from the charnel house of modern Vietnam, she was completing the circuit begun centuries earlier, even as, when the President threw the switch that ignited the torch, he was acting, however ceremoniously, merely in the capacity of a diligent lighthouse keeper.

For those of us of, shall we say, pre-modern aesthetic temperament, the parade of sailing vessels was The Main Event. I do not think I am slighting the Great Lady whose birthday facelift prompted the occasion, because symbolically the ships were inseparable from the event. How else could the exiles have arrived, save by them? They were intrinsic, not extraneous to the event, and if the staff of the *New Republic* thought they too were gaudy, then I say phooey.

The commentators did not, mercifully, repair to John Masefield every five minutes, except for the obligatory prolegomenon about going down to the sea again. I would have liked a coda or two from Herman Melville, who was born just a few feet from the harbor and who ended his days as a customs inspector on the same island where President Reagan presided over the ceremonies. It was there, around the Battery, that Ishmael, afflicted with that "damp, drizzly November in my soul" had resolved upon medicine that even Sigmund Freud would have overlooked, accounting it "high time to get to sea. . . . There is nothing surprising in all this," he tells us. "If they but knew it, almost all men in their degree, some time or other, cherish very nearly the same feelings towards the ocean with me."

And who among us did not feel that way with Ishmael last July 4th as we watched that stately waterborne parade celebrated in this volume. One commentator remarked from Battery Park that she was surprised that the crowd did not seem in more of a "party mood." The atmosphere, she said, was more "reverential." (Possibly some were suffering the after-effects of the Big Party the night before, but in this meditation I prefer to think that it was reverence that had o'ercome them all.)

We are, from time to time, reminded that New York is a harbor. I say this not at all lightly. Having replaced Paris and London as the cultural center of the world (Tokyo apparently has become its fi-

nancial center), we have become accustomed to thinking of the city in terms of art, medicine, restaurants, politics, crime, Philip Johnson skyscrapers, unfinished subways, AIDS, Broadway, campaigns-to-clean-up-Times-Square and all the rest; but how often do we think of it in its maritime context? The days of the great ocean liners are over, the unions and the mob have driven most waterfront business away to more complaisant harbors. True, the South Street Sea-

port has been renovated and boutiqued; but it is only episodically that we are reminded that this harbor, where Henry Hudson fetched up in his small ship the *Half Moon* in 1609, was truly, as one of his officers wrote in the log, "a very good place to fall in with."

The parade of Tall Ships was an epiphany on a grand scale, a reminder that not only New York, but this entire nation is an island. Epiphanies are by definition larger-than-life, and the press is forgiven for having been moved to larger-than-life rhapsodies. One television correspondent, aboard one of the Tall Ships, was so moved by the sensation as to tell us that it gave him a feeling "almost of floating". I confess that I got so caught up by the majesty and in what one of my sailing companions calls the yo-ho-ho of the nautical life that I found myself acquiescing in the correspondent's observation, until it occurred to me that the sensation of floating, if you are aboard a boat, is perhaps not so mystical as all that. Maybe you just had to be there.

But oh what a parliament of masts it was, to use Melville's description of what lower Manhattan used to look like. There are only 30-odd Tall Ships left, and twenty-three of them turned out for the occasion, some having crossed the Atlantic just to be there. In the Fiberglass Era, to see one such ship on the horizon is event enough, but to see over twenty of them all in a line, topsails set, their crews standing sentinel high above the decks was almost too much to absorb. From the air the spectacle was of a vast, peaceable armada— some 40,000 boats!—but from sea level, watching the parade's progress through the sun-pierced mist thrown up by the fireboats, it was a scene out of J.M.W. Turner. You could not see the enormous hull of the 295-foot-long Coast Guard bark *Eagle,* only her masts and 21,000 square feet of sail framed by the gigantic jets of water from the fireboats, each of these moving fountains shooting 20,000 gallons of water per minute into the air, enough to fill a small swimming pool. Was any emperor's triumphal entry into Rome proceeded by a more dazzling honor guard? (I will answer that, thank you: No.)

For that matter, was any Roman Triumph itself more breath-catching than the procession that sailed past Governor's Island that Friday morning? The *Eagle*—originally the German Ship *Horst Wessel*, and credited with shooting down three Allied planes during World War II—followed by the Norwegian *Christian Radich*, the Argentine *Libertad*, the *Danmark*, the *Simon Bolivar*, the *Esmeralda*. Ten years earlier I had sailed from Santo Domingo to New York aboard the *Libertad*, and caused my hosts no small consternation by climbing all the way up one of her masts, which experience had left me a) profoundly grateful not to have been born a 19th-century crewman and b) sad not to have been atop my old perch, nearly eyeball to eyeball with the verdigris goddess that was at the center of all the attention.

It is the small image that fixes itself in the memory. I am thinking of the *Spirit of Massachusetts*, replica of one of the old Grand Banks fishing schooners, towing that dory in her wake. It was the seafaring equivalent of the riderless horse with the boots reversed in the stirrups. A few months before, the man who had been the *Massachusetts*'s first captain had gone down with his ship, the *Pride of Baltimore*, after she had been capsized by a terrible wave in a sudden blow of a white squall. There amidst the pomp, the horns, the blimps, the fireboats, and the banners, one ship was paying simple homage to a gone shipmate.

There was much lamenting that day of the fact that the great age of sail had passed. It is unlikely that we will see another such sight this side of heaven, but consoling to know that as the age of great ships has passed, the American Age has not. How could one doubt that a nation capable of throwing itself such a celebration is capable of keeping the beacon lit, the dream alive, for ages yet to come?

CHALLENGE
OF
THE SEA

To the delight of millions, to the bewilderment of some, the return of the Tall Ships in tribute to Lady Liberty was a spectacular event spectacularly staged and assiduously promoted. The very sight of the lithe white-winged birds of the sea was moving to most observers, stirring memories of childhood dreams and aspirations, perhaps evoking nostalgia for an apparently simpler world.

Certainly, the controlled ballet of huge and heavy ships slicing through the water somehow gave visual expression to one of mankind's most ancient desires: skimming into New York harbor, tested by the ocean's deadly calms and thundering rages, each sleek craft was a symbol of courage and ingenuity in the face of Nature's ancient challenges. Dangerous, unpredictable, the seas have been traversed, if not mastered. Strong, graceful, the ships designed and sailed by generations of sailors have defied the elements, breaking the bonds that once tied us forever to the lands where we were born.

For that reason alone, it was altogether proper that celebration of the nation's preeminent symbol of freedom and opportunity was linked with the tactile poetry of the Tall Ships. After the U.S. Civil War and well into our own century, untold hundreds of thousands of immigrants fled oppression, starvation and social rigidity on the enormous square-riggers typical of late 19th-century shipping.

To many ancestors of the millions of Americans who joined in the festivities on July 4, the ships waiting in a European port may well have promised escape from despair, a flight toward hope. The crossing itself, however, could become an ordeal for all but the most physically fit and emotionally strong.

First, there would have been overcrowding, poor ventilation and only the most rudimentary facilities. Passengers, who probably carried with them their entire store of worldly possessions, were also required to feed themselves during the two or three weeks of the voyage. Upon boarding, they were inspected to see that enough foodstuffs and cooking fuel had been brought. Crew members were surly and abusive, particularly when the awestruck landlubbers stepped on ropes lying about or ignorantly blocked a sweating worker's path.

There was a strict routine aboard. Passengers were to rise at 7 in the morning, dress, roll up their bedding and get to work sweeping the decks and throwing wastes and dirt overboard. Inspection was typically frequent and demanding. The quarters were generally rough wooden bunks built very close together in the cargo hatch of a ship traveling empty westward to pick up timber. The comfort, safety and mental well-being of passengers were not felt to be the concern of the ship's master and crew.

The professional sailor's contempt for passengers was not without foundation, of course. Those unfamiliar with the demands of the sea and life aboard ship could themselves be dangerous. In 1848, passengers on the *Ocean Monarch* tried to boil water for tea as the ship set out from Liverpool. Fire raced through the vessel, and 178 of the 338 emigrants on board died as she sank into the Mersey.

But even as passengers in the cramped, close hold stumbled through a fetid darkness ill-lit by occasional flickering lamps, their discomfort may have been eclipsed by the terrors, real or imagined, of transatlantic travel in a rolling creaking ship on a tossing, angry sea. Consider that many immigrants to America were poor farmers and unemployed laborers and their families. Most may never have even seen the ocean, much less found their sea legs in one of the mammoth Atlantic storms that can seem to tear the horizon apart.

Perhaps worst of all, at least in the recollection of

the seamen who made their lives upon the sea, was the horrific noise of a big blow in full fury. In the memoirs, doughty old captains recall winds roaring like freight trains, masts groaning as if about to snap in two, the shrieks and whistles of the rigging, the shuddering of the entire vessel as heavy seas washed over the decks or slammed into the sides. If seamen kept their nerve, it was because they were busy saving the ship as their ears thrummed with "that almost indescribable cacophony, the song of driven sail."

Passengers, for the most part, could do little but huddle below and pray. No doubt many suffered sea-sickness, even on the calm days. Not a fatal malady, *mal de mer* generally sparks rough joking from those not affected, but the victim's sufferings are real and intense. The body goes completely out of sync. Nausea ebbs and flows uncontrollably, and the balance dissipates upon an inner world as watery as the insistently rocking swells below

ship. Some become so distraught, in fact, that they try to throw themselves overboard. Meanwhile, life-threatening illnesses could sweep through the confined quarters. Thousands of would-be immigrants died at sea from cholera, ship-fever and typhus. In 1846, to take one documented example, 106,000 Scots and Irish immigrants headed toward America and Canada; of that total, 12,200 died on board ship or upon arrival, and the next few weeks after landing saw the deaths of 7,000 more. Loss of life was also a function of shipowner greed. Overcrowding was the reason for the sinking of many of the fifty-nine ships that were lost in the North Atlantic from 1847 to 1853.

Yet the ordeals, the threat of death, were instantly forgotten, we can imagine, when the barometer rose, the sun came out to make the grey-green waters sparkle blue again, and the winds blew strong but steady, filling the thousands of squares of white sail full to bursting. Then,

there were songs and gossip and romance on deck. The mild salt spray felt bracing and clean on skin that had not been bathed for days. Fresh air swept away the clinging odors of steerage. Now, the constantly working sailors may have seemed to have a touch of the heroic. If they could seem indifferent or worse to their charges in port, the rigors of the crossing would prove that they were skilled, tough, loyal to the fraternity of the ship. Perhaps the occasional passenger discovered the surprising sentimentality that could lurk beneath the gruff, grizzled exterior; when it came to the ship herself, many who worked her felt something between reverence and desire.

In fact, the men who sailed the great square-riggers of the sixty-year period when sail was supreme in the late 19th and early 20th centuries were, not unlike the immigrants to America, seekers of opportunity and greater freedom. Europe's social and economic problems were reflected in more than one way upon the decks of the sailing vessels; immigrants and seamen alike shared the need to make new lives for themselves, no matter what the costs in lost family ties and nostalgia for the land of one's birth. To us, the life of the sea may seem harsh, unrewardingly dangerous and financially disappointing. Often, the alternative would have been the grinding poverty of Dickensian slums or the drudgery of ill-paid labor on someone else's farm. Whatever the sea may have offered as thrill, adventure and the exotic, to most seamen it offered first and foremost a job.

The men who went "down to the sea in ships" began as very young boys, beardless and skinny and unlearned. Some were terrified, others wide-eyed and eager, but they would not last if they were not remarkably determined, quick to learn, resilient and hard-working. Within the first two months, for example, an apprentice was expected to learn the names and precise functions of 300 different ropes and become able to race to the right

one, if necessary, at the height of a gale in the dead of night.

Work was constant, wearying, perhaps confusing. The fatigued young sailor was only barely restored by the ship's diet, which was based upon wormy salt pork and ship's biscuit. The cook, who produced cracker hash, slumgullion, dandyfunk, burgoo and salt junk, was always known, not surprisingly, as "Slushy". Water, which was stored in large wooden casks, became stale and distinctly unpalatable as the voyage progressed, unless one was fortunate enough to work the large steel ships that carried a distillation unit. At the end of the day, if the weather did not require work aloft, the seamen would collapse on his "donkey's breakfast", a straw-filled mattress.

Mistakes could earn a sharp reprimand or severe punishment from a superior. Not infrequently, a hapless young sailor would be sentenced to stay alone up on the foremast crosstrees during a winter storm. Some were brought down dead. In one infamous incident, a captain confined an apprentice to the ship's hencoop for five months, not even allowing him out to scrape off hen droppings.

But the mistakes that earned punishment from man were preferable to mistakes that could flip a boy into the water or send him smashing into the deck. The poetry in motion of the great sails could be mortal music indeed to the unwary or unskilled sailor. A sudden shift in the weather might mean that many of the huge sails had to be quickly furled. Crew had to scramble up the rigging, hand over hand, to the highest yards, the spars from which the sails hung. In unison with his fellows, a sailor had to loose the flapping canvas, while maintaining a precarious balance perhaps 150 feet or more above a swaying deck. The ancient rule was one hand for the ship, one for the sailor. In actual practice, spurred by the growing threat of a storm, the crew might work with both hands, depending on their sea-steady feet and the wind at their backs for support.

The task was exhausting. The heavy, whipping sail had to be wrapped tightly around the yard. In freezing rain, fog or the fiercest gales, the struggle was excruciating. One slip on the wet or icing ropes, and death was likely. Yet the pressure to do the job was so intense that fear was not often conscious. One sailor recalled being knocked from his footing when a sudden gust blew the sail against him. By extreme good luck, he landed in the rigging several yards below. Without thinking, he scrambled back up to his post, the fall unnoticed by his companions. Only later, when he was back on deck, warming his frozen hand, and the job was completed, did terror seize him.

Statistics were not carefully kept, but it was a rare ship that did not lose at least a couple of seamen on a long and difficult voyage. The man tossed overboard had a slightly better chance, if the weather was manageable, than someone who fell to the deck. But in darkness or heavy mist, or when it took up to an hour to bring the ship around, the man in the water was inevitably lost.

Such a violent and lonely death would have been harrowing but relatively swift. Perhaps even more terrifying was the disaster that downed a ship and led to the loss of all lives aboard. In the frigid reaches of the seas, an iceberg could slide inexorably into the hull, splintering or mortally wounding the grandest of vessels. Monster storms could de-mast a ship, leaving her to drift onto killer reefs or rocky shoals. A freak calm upon the waters could idle a schooner for weeks, dooming

her crew to die of thirst and starvation under
cruelly fair skies. Green seas surging across the
decks could hurl men into the maw of giant waves,
and the weight of such a surge, perhaps hundreds
of tons, could capsize the greatest of the sailing
ships. Death might eventually come only after
hours or days of blood-chilling fear, or enervating
toil. Numb from cold, fatigue and despair, the seamen may have found release at least in the arms of
the restive sea. She had won.

But the victories against the most powerful
storms were legion, the stuff of song and fireside

tales. And the faces that appear in fading photos from the late 19th century do not show the ravages of a miserable life. True, the boys fill out quickly, their bodies harden and they have the air and solidity of men five or ten years older. Yet theirs is a proud, half-humorous toughness, not the look of children worn down before their time. They are survivors, initiates in an ancient and demanding craft. We can see why their relatives felt the sea had "made a man" out of a boy, but what kind of men did she create?

From all accounts, the best seamen could give their all to team-work when necessary and, as if in reaction, become memorably individual, if not downright idiosyncratic, when relaxing. They could flinch and then go on, when a friend was suddenly and violently killed. They were also famously sentimental, easily touched by the glow of the dawn in the tropics or by a simple ditty about the girls left behind in port. They brawled, and they prayed. They met the races of the world, ate its strange variety of foods and came home perhaps once a year, if that. For most of them, true "home" became the mercurial ocean herself. It was upon a ship, and in the work of a ship, that these men were distinct from other men. They became strangers to the land.

No one more fully represented life at sea than the captain. Although there was the occasional fool, misfit or larcenous rogue, the typical master of a tall ship was of necessity a considerable human being. He had to hold the respect of the crew, not a few of whom might have more actual sailing experience than he. He would be honored if he was fair, beloved if he was wise, feared if he expected a crew member's best. Most important, however, was that he know how to sail a huge, complicated machine in all possible conditions. He must, as one master put it, "prepare thoroughly for the fight beforehand." His mistakes would cost lives. With little warning, he had to supervise the

trimming of sails, judging how best to ride out a gale or take advantage of a wind. Because each decision would take hours to execute as sailors fought with sails on the rigging, he had to have an almost infernal sense of what the weather would do next. No radio or other technical device gave him advance information. If he misjudged, and the crew had to reverse their hard work in order to keep the ship going, he was likely to earn resentment, if not contempt. Ultimately, he was responsible for the comforts of his men, down to their daily diet, and for the condition of the ship, protecting the sizable investment of her owners. In matters large and small, he was the final arbiter, and not only at sea. When the ship made port, he had to deal with the local authorities and their sometimes questionably creative fees, taxes and other charges. He had to bargain with dock-workers, traders, shippers; he had to be a shrewd businessman, adept politician and staunch symbol of authority. He had, in short, to be damned sure he knew what he was doing.

Understandably, for a successful captain life aboard ship was not without comfort. His quarters on a cargo schooner might resemble in every detail the Victorian or Edwardian drawing room of a well-to-do American or European businessman. Period photos show such amenities as marble fireplaces, beveled mirrors, stylish wicker with plush or leather seats and backs, carved mahogany chairs and roll-top desks. Brass fittings shine, and the dark wooden walls of the rooms richly oiled. Captains brought their wives and children aboard, perhaps further reinforcing their image as father of the ship. Presumably, board members of the shipping company were not unaware of the psychological advantage of allowing a captain's loved ones aboard; he would have all the more to protect.

After all, we must not forget that, despite the elegance of the tall ships and the drama of the great sails in full flight, the business of the vessels was

business. They carried cargo, and that cargo was generally heavy, difficult to deal with, and occasionally threatening to life and limb. A hold stuffed with wool, for example, could blaze afire spontaneously. Fire at sea affords no escape, and the wind acts as a natural bellows. Even more startling as a danger, at least to the lay observer, was a cargo of rice. Wet by washing of storm surges or leaks, the rice would swell implacably, bursting the hull like a plaything of matchsticks. The ship would immediately sink.

Still cargo was the mother's milk of the sailing fleets, particularly after steam appeared and took the passenger business away. In the dying days of commercial cargo sail, the largest carriers set off on voyages that could last as long as two years. The average ship could hold 3,000 tons of goods; that would the equivalent of about 60,000 sacks of grain.

It was for reasons of trade that the French government, for example, subsidized the construction and operation of 212 new windjammers from 1892 through 1902. The great age of sail was, first and foremost, a great age of international trade. In Europe, there was a market hungry for the seemingly inexhaustible supplies of timber to be found in the American Northwest. The relative prosperity of late 19th-century "Victorians" throughout western Europe demanded more foodstuffs and coal from Australia, halfway around the world. The continuing development of the industrial economies also required coal, as well as such raw materials as copper ore from Chile. It became obvious to shipbuilders in this period that speed for these cargoes was less important to the profit-minded than capacity and durability. The mandate was simple: stuff as much as possible into a ship that would bludgeon its way safely home. The idea was to produce veritable warehouses that could be depended upon to float from continent to continent.

Despite a commonly held assumption, it is not precisely true that the coming of steamships gave a sudden death blow to the tall ships. At first, the square-riggers could usually best the speeds of steam-powered craft, often making an average of seven knots. To the shipper, it was also no small thing that wind power is free, whereas coal could be expensive, particularly in ports far from home. Inflation was a function of distance. And steam power required fresh water for the boilers. Therefore, even as the new ships were designed for greater speed, sail held on to monopolies in many markets around the world. And the speed of the square-riggers remained formidable, if not supreme. One cargo carrier, in a particularly famous episode, made 20.75 knots, only slightly less than the all-time record speed of 21 knots set by a clipper ship, one of the legendary sailing vessels built primarily for speed. The best average speeds of clipper ships over a day-long run of several hundred miles had been 18 and 19 knots, but the German five-masted windjammer *Potosi* racked up an average of just under 16 knots in a day's run of 378 miles. (For the reader unfamiliar with speeds in the water, it may be easier to visualize 21 knots, say, as about 34 feet per second—swift passage, indeed for the huge and often overloaded square-riggers.) Or, to take a longer view, heavily loaded windjammers were known to make the trip from London to Melbourne, Australia, in just over two months.

Speed was born of wind, of course, and there were upper limits of safety, because an overcanvassed vessel (that is, one with her full suit of sails unfurled) was susceptible to several kinds of disaster. The sails could be blown to tatters, the mast toppled, or the entire ship either capsized or literally pushed underwater. When the winds surpassed 40 knots, the uppermost sails would be furled. Others would be taken in as a gale increased in force until, at about 70 knots, the only sails still catching the wind would be the lower spanker, the lowest staysails and the lower top-sails. These were necessary to keep the ship on a forward course.

Unwieldly as this kind of locomotion might seem, it bested steam for many years on certain long cargo voyages, for only the heavy but surprisingly resilient square-riggers could fight their way around the southern tips of Africa and South America, where the winds blow eternally and waves are not unusually 50 feet from trough to crest. The more daunting water coursed around Cape Horn, where square-riggers sailed for the lucrative trade in nitrate, or guano, the natural fertilizer found along the rocky shores of Chile and Peru. Also, there was a brief and brisk passenger trade there during the California Gold Rush. In 1849 alone, 800 ships crammed with gold-fevered adventurers plowed through the legendary "greybeards" that foam in the thunderously stormy waters know as the "forties", because of their latitude. Even ship's pumps capable of discharging a ton of water a minute from below decks were hard pressed in gales down at the Horn. More than once, a vessel had to struggle for as long as two months to round this famous obstacle and slip at last from one contending ocean into the other. How many ships were lost, and how many men died? No one knows, but the total of the former was surely in the hundreds, and the latter must have been thousands.

But one man's vision changed all that. In 1869, Ferdinand de Lesseps realized his dream of completing the Suez Canal, effectively halving the distance from Europe to the ports of the East. "I apologize to the sailing vessels", he was later to write, for they could not be maneuvered through the canal; there was little wind, and the channels were narrow. And so it was that by the onset of the Great War, no significant cargo trade was carried by sail. The fleet birds of the sea lost their wings, and, as the Opsail Celebration showed us this year, few were to survive into our own day.

PRIDE OF BALTIMORE

*The tragic sinking of the **Pride of Baltimore** was a startling reminder of the vulnerability of sail, even in the technological age. The agile two-mast schooner, built in 1977 to resemble the swift 19th-century Baltimore clippers, was diesel-powered and equipped with contemporary communications equipment. Nonetheless, when a "downburst" struck her without warning in heavy seas north of Puerto Rico May 14, she was immediately toppled. (A downburst is a sudden descent of cold air that hits water and causes a violent shift in prevailing wind direction, much like the wind shear associated with several airplane accidents in recent years.) The crew of twelve was thrown into the waves and, no more than sixty seconds afterward, the ship was gone. Lost with her were the captain and three members of the crew; the survivors were rescued from her life raft five days later by a Norwegian tanker. The 136-foot-long schooner, recognizable by her sharply raked masts, had been christened to recall the popular nickname of the **Chasseur**, a Baltimore clipper that captured eighteen British ships during the blockade of the War of 1812. Hand-built for $400,000 as a goodwill ambassador for the city, **Pride of Baltimore** was beautifully crafted of such tropical hardwoods as bullettree, Santa Maria and Machich, as well as longleaf yellow pine, Douglas fir and rosewood. Capable of crossing the Atlantic in forty days, she had logged more than 135,000 miles in voyages to more than 140 ports of call in the coastal states of the U.S. and twenty-six foreign countries.*

Classification of sailboats

Staysail schooner

Brigantine

Three-masted staysail schooner

Jib-headed ketch

Bark

Barkentine

Jib-headed cutter

Yawl

Brig

Full-rigged ship

SAILS OF A FOUR-MASTED BARK

1. Bowsprit
2. Martingale
3. Figurehead
4. Flying jib
5. Outer jib
6. Inner jib
7. Fore topmast staysail

8. Foremast
9. Fore royal
10. Fore upper topgallant sail
11. Fore lower topgallant sail
12. Fore upper topsail
13. Fore lower topsail
14. Foresail, Fore course

15. Main royal staysail
16. Main topgallant staysail
17. Main middle staysail
18. Main topmast staysail
19. Mainmast
20. Main royal
21. Main upper topgallant sail

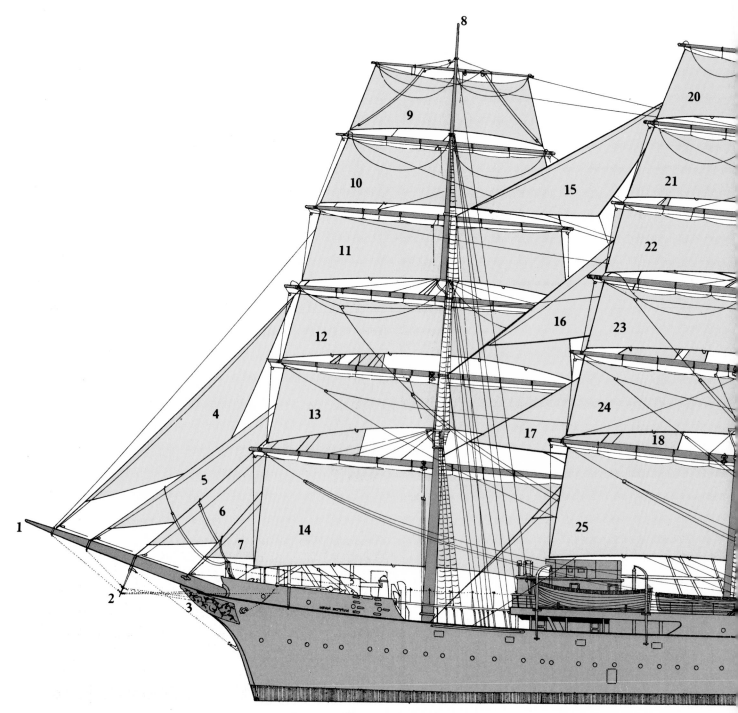

22. Main lower topgallant sail
23. Main upper topsail
24. Main lower topsail
25. Mainsail, Main course
26. Mizzen royal staysail
27. Mizzen topgallant staysail
28. Mizzen middle staysail
29. Mizzen topmast staysail
30. Mizzen mast
31. Mizzen royal
32. Mizzen upper topgallant sail
33. Mizzen lower topgallant sail
34. Mizzen upper topsail
35. Mizzen lower topsail
36. Crossjack, Mizzen course
37. Jigger topgallant staysail
38. Jigger topmast staysail
39. Jigger staysail
40. Jigger mast
41. Gaff topsail
42. Spanker

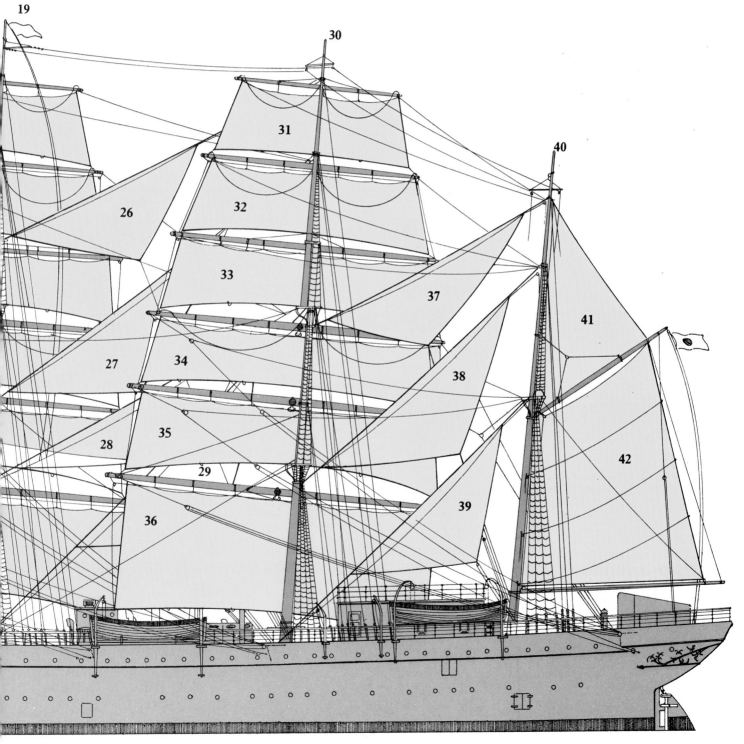

THE
TALL SHIPS

AMERIGO VESPUCCI

Softly glowing against dark skies before July 4, the 330-foot-long **Amerigo Vespucci,** *largest sailing ship based in the Mediterranean, was built in 1930 for training officer cadets at the Italian Naval Academy at Livorno. Steel-hulled, with two square-rigged masts 160 feet tall, she was designed wide and high-sided like a 19th-century frigate in order to accommodate up to 500*

officers, crew and students. Lovingly maintained, she boasts elegantly furnished ward rooms and a life-size figurehead of her namesake, the Italian explorer of South America whose name was given to the entire New World in 1507. Though not a swift racer, she is an eye-catching spectator at sailing events and has used her unusual beauty on educational tours to warn of growing pollution in the seas.

BELEM

France's official representative in the Salute to Liberty, the **Belem,** built in 1896 for trade with South America and the West Indies, usually rests in the Seine near the Eiffel Tower, where tourists flock to learn her remarkable history. She has served as a pleasure yacht for the Duke of Westminster and for the rich Irish brewer, A.E. Guinness, who sailed her around the globe. From 1952 to 1976, she was a training ship for Italian cadets. In 1979, thanks to public interest and seed money from The National Union of Savings Banks of France, she was brought back home. By 1985, the 572-ton bark was fully restored to sailing condition.

BLUENOSE II

Canada's **Bluenose II** is a 1963 replica of a treasured national symbol, a Nova Scotia Grand Banks fishing schooner, built in 1921, that won the International Fishermen's Cup Races between the U.S. and Canada every summer from then until 1938. Sold to a West Indian freighting company during World War II, she was totally wrecked on a coral reef near Haiti in 1946. As "Queen of the North Atlantic", the lovely veteran is recalled not only by this accurate replica but by her image on the reverse of the Canadian dime. Her daughter, **Bluenose II,** does not race but acts as goodwill ambassador for Nova Scotia, whose fishermen were dubbed "bluenoses" by their fiercest rivals, the fishermen of Gloucester, Massachusetts, because of a blue-skinned potato grown in the province.

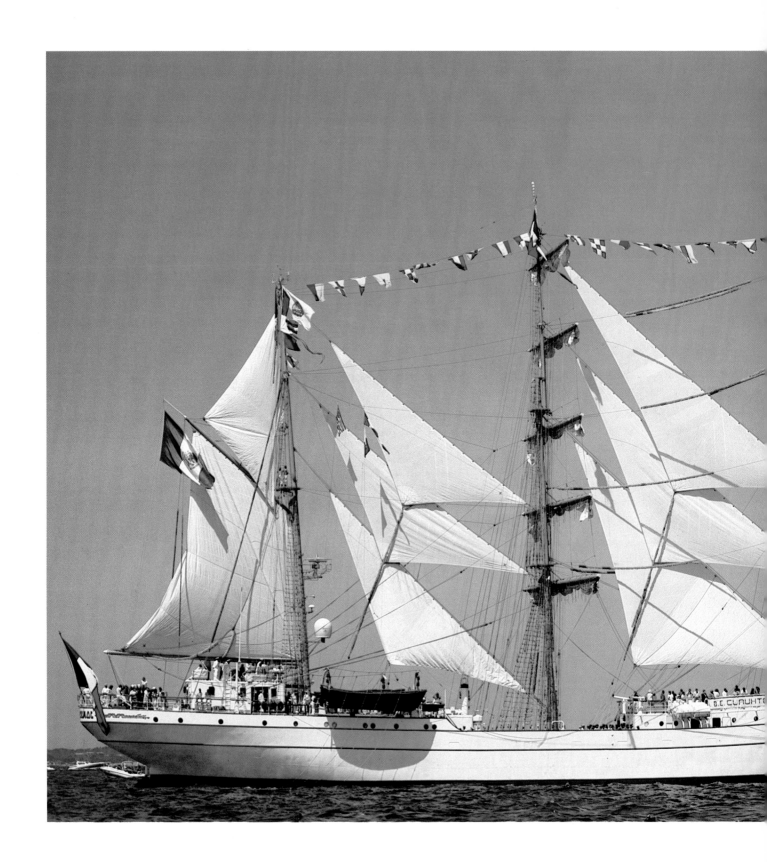

CUAUHTEMOC

Youngest of the tall ships, Mexico's sleek **Cuauhtemoc** (pronounced coo-OUT-ay-mock), paraded with some of her approximately 25,000 square feet of sails furled. Launched in 1982 and based in Veracruz, she is the schoolship of the Mexican Naval Academy and keeps her complement of 185 unusually busy with an extensive yearly cruise schedule. Cuauhtemoc, last free ruler of the ancient Aztecs, courageously resisted Spanish might but was murdered by the conquerors in 1524.

CAPITAN MIRANDA

*Built as a sailing cargo carrier in 1930, long after most such ships had vanished from commercial use, Uruguay's **Capitan Miranda** eventually had her rig removed and was employed in trade as a power vessel after World War II. The splendidly modern schooner rig she sports now, based upon a design developed half a century ago for racing yachts, was added when the Uruguayan Navy commissioned her as a training schoolship in 1978. Many Americans remember the **Capitan Miranda**'s participation that very year in the Tall Ships Pacific conclave on the West Coast, but her complement of 40 cadets and 45 crew members generally cruises the South Atlantic.*

CHRISTIAN RADICH

A frequent victor in international races, Norway's fleet Christian Radich (pronounced RAH-dik) is named for the wealthy ship owner who subsidized her construction for the Oslo Schoolship Association in 1937. During World War II, Germany impressed her into service as a submarine depot ship when Norway refused to cooperate in using her as a training vessel in the Baltic. At

war's end, she was discovered capsized at Flensburg, Germany, missing masts and yards. After two years of extensive refitting back home, she was launched for service in Norway's Merchant Marine in 1947. Perhaps 35,000 Americans visited her when she docked for three days on an unusual trip to Chicago in 1976. She gave such pleasure that when a severe north Atlantic storm later ripped her sails to shreds, the people who had seen her in Chicago and at other Great Lakes port cities contributed enough money to replace her 13,280 feet of sail.

DANMARK

*Launched in 1932 to train officers for the Danish Merchant Navy, the steel-hulled, double-bottomed **Danmark** was destined to have a significant impact upon U.S. military training. Visiting the New York World's Fair when war broke out in 1939, she and her crew were offered to the Coast Guard. Over 5,000 cadets were trained at New London, Connecticut, in a program so effec-*

*tive that the service was inspired to take Germany's **Horst Wessel** and commission it as the **Eagle.** Modernization in 1959 cut the **Danmark**'s capacity from 120 cadets to eighty. The 250-foot full-rigged ship regularly visits the East Coast of the U.S. on one of two annually scheduled cruises. Captain Wilhelm Hansen, 69, most experienced of the Tall Ships helmsmen, retired this year after half a century at sea, including 22 years in charge of the **Danmark.***

DEWA RUCI

Training ship for Indonesia, where sailing schooners are still in use for cargo runs, the **Dewa Ruci** (pronounced day-wah-ROO-chi) is named for a deity of the sea in the Hindu epic "The Mahabarata". Usually cruising in East Asian waters, the steel-hulled brigantine is fully air-conditioned. Her visit to OpSail '86 was the high point of a global circumnavigation for her complement of forty Indonesian Navy cadets, fifty-one crew members and eleven officers. Built in 1953, the trim **Dewa Ruci** is similar to the **Jadran,** built in 1932 as a training ship for the Yugoslav Navy.

ELISSA

Texans and other U.S. sailing aficionados raised a special cheer when **Elissa** appeared in the 4-mile-long Parade of Sail. Docked as a museum ship in Galveston since 1979 and lovingly restored to her original condition, the fine iron-hulled bark was originally built in Scotland in 1877. After almost a century of service sailing under British, Norwegian, Swedish and Finnish flags, she was converted to power and was delivering cargo in the Greek islands when the Galveston Historical Foundation bought her in 1975. The 160-foot-long **Elissa** is typical of the tough little 19th-century ships that successfully sailed the world time and again.

49

EAGLE

Shown gliding past the famed Chrysler Building, at left, the U.S. Coast Guard's flagship **Eagle,** *host ship for Operation Sail 1986 as in 1964 and 1976, causes some raised eyebrows among traditionalists with her bold identifying stripe. Originally built in 1936 by Germany and commissioned the* **Horst Wessel,** *she is the nearly identical sister ship of three contemporaries now*

owned by other nations—the **Sagres II** of Portugal, the **Tovaritsch II** of the U.S.S.R., the **Mircea** of Rumania. Designated a supply vessel during World War II, she is supposed to have shot down at least three Russian planes in the Baltic. Today, all Coast Guard trainees spend time on the **Eagle;** her schedule includes two five-week-long and three one-week cruises every summer.

Here, by the towers of your splendid town,
Ship after ship, the Racers will come in,
Their colours going up and their sails down,
As welcomes to America begin.
The sirens will all bellow and make din
And all bells beat, in thunder of ovation,
As, one by one, each Racer, each a Queen,
Arrives, salutes the EAGLE and takes station,
One beauty more in all the lovely scene,
The Grand scene, of the ships that have made good
Their path across the sea by hardihood . . . .

John Masefield, Poet Laureate of England
1964

ESMERALDA

The world's second largest sailing ship, Chile's **Esmeralda,** 353 feet long with a mast height of 165 feet, has frequently circumnavigated the globe since her launching in 1952. The four-mast barkentine, capable of twelve knots under engine power, is armed with a quartet of 5.7 centimeter rapid fire guns and carries eighteen officers, a crew of ninety-nine and up to 233 cadets training with the Chilean Naval Academy. Her name, Spanish for "emerald", honors a beloved national symbol, a warship captured from Spain in 1818 during the struggle for independence and used victoriously against Peru and Bolivia in the 1879 Nitrate War. The graceful craft, suggestive of the four-mast cargo schooners familiar along U.S. coasts after the turn of the century, was at the storm center of a very contemporary conflict when protesters at Liberty Weekend charged that she had been used by the Pinochet government in 1973 for interrogation and torture of alleged dissidents.

JUAN SEBASTIAN de ELCANO

*Elder sister to the **Esmeralda** but rigged as a schooner with a fore gaff-sail, the Spanish Navy's training ship, **Juan Sebastian de Elcano,** has charged the seas since 1927, carrying a complement of 407, including 210 cadets. Her name honors the Spanish skipper who was first to circle the globe, safely bringing home the only ship to survive Magellan's doomed five-ship expedi-*

tion of 1519–23. She herself has gone round the world six times. With a mainmast height of 164 feet, she is one of the twenty-two tall ships unable to sail under the Brooklyn Bridge and other East River spans.

GLORIA

*First of a new generation of tall ships especially designed for cadet training, Colombia's remarkably beautiful **Gloria**, launched from Bilbao, Spain, in 1968, recalls the classic German barks built in the 1920s and 1930s. Her sister ships include Ecuador's **Guayas**, Venezuela's **Simon Bolivar** and the **Cuauhtemoc** of Mexico; all joined **Gloria** in OpSail '86. Recognizable by the large enclosed pilothouse forward of the mizzenmast, she is renowned for a crew that will take to the yards and sing national songs in unison.*

LIBERTAD

*With sails furled for the 6-hour-long round trip of the Parade, Argentina's **Libertad,** though one of the world's largest tall ships with a 3,675-ton displacement, is also swift, having once crossed the Atlantic at an average speed of eighteen knots. Launched in 1956, she annually takes up to 120 four-year cadets on lengthy training cruises, frequently stopping in foreign ports and participating in worldwide gatherings of sailing ships. With a mainmast 163 feet high and a sail area of 28,450 square feet, she evokes the legendary vessels of old while making use of 20th-century knowledge of design and technology.*

SAGRES II

*Immediately recognizable from the ten giant red Portuguese Crosses of Christ billowing on her sails, **Sagres II** was, like her sister ship the **Eagle,** built by Germany in the 1930's as a training ship. Originally named the **Albert Leo Schlageter,** she suffered severe mine damage during use as a supply vessel in the Baltic in World War II. Seized by the U.S. and given to Brazil in 1948, she was known as the **Guanabara** until Portugal bought her in 1961 to replace an aging cadet ship, the **Sagres I.** Her figurehead is Prince Henry the Navigator, the great royal patron of oceanic exploration and founder of the world's first college of navigation who died in 1460 at Sagres, the port in southern Portugal from which many daring sea voyages were launched in the 15th century.*

GAZELA OF PHILADELPHIA

Heir to a 500-year Portuguese tradition, the **Gazela of Philadelphia,** built in 1883, was still fishing the Grand Banks for cod in 1969, when she was the last of the country's square-rigged fishing schooners to be retired. Now, she is probably the oldest and largest wood-hulled square-rigger still actively plying the waves. Most of her hull's oak and pine is original, having been harvested from a forest especially planted in 1460 by Prince Henry the Navigator. Owned by the Penn's Landing Corporation of Philadelphia, she is sailed and maintained by enthusiastic volunteers.

POGORIA

Her foresails sporting the striking symbol of her owner, Poland's Iron Shackle Fraternity, the **Pogoria** represented Canada's West Island College Class Afloat Programme at OpSail '86. Capable of up to 200 miles a day, the ship was launched in 1980 and has since sailed through the waters of the sub-Antarctic islands and circumnavigated the globe. In an unusual and successful experiment, costs for the Class Afloat trainee sailing cruises have been supplemented by the addition of paying guests.

GUAYAS

Her men standing proudly in the rigging, the 914-ton **Guayas,** built in 1977, is a training ship for the Ecuadoran Navy and was christened in honor of an 1841 steamship, the first to be constructed in South America. As a participant in the 1980 Tall Ships Races, she earned the American Sail Training Association Cutty Sark Trophy for international friendship. Based in Guayaquil, the 257-foot-long three-mast bark carries eighty cadets under the guidance of thirty-five officers and experienced crew.

SHABAB OMAN

A barkentine commissioned by the Sultan of Oman in 1979 as **Shabab Oman** *("Youth of Oman" in Arabic), this graceful three-mast ship made a rare crossing of the Atlantic to participate in OpSail '86. From home base on the Arabian Sea, she generally takes naval training cruises to the ports of the Persian Gulf, Pakistan and India. En route to New York, her complement of thirty midshipmen was twice replaced, giving ninety young cadets from many walks of life a glimpse of the challenge of sail.*

SIMON BOLIVAR

Lady Liberty gazes upon Venezuela's superbly designed and built **Simon Bolivar,** *which, though launched as recently as 1979, has become a familiar participant in Tall Ships events. Her frequent transatlantic voyages and tours of ports in the Americas have gained a wide following for this class "A" square-rigger, exclusively used as a training vessel for the Venezuelan Navy. Eighteen women were among the eighty-four cadets aboard during OpSail '86.*

SØRLANDET

*Her sails fully unfurled in the Parade, the 559-ton **Sørlandet** ("Southern Land" in Norwegian) is owned now by the Full-rigged Ship Sørlandet Non-Profit Foundation, which sponsors training cruises for applicants not necessarily interested in a career at sea. Trainees, from both sexes, can be from any country. Built in 1927 with funds donated by a Norwegian ship owner, A. O. T. Skjelbred, who specified that no auxiliary power be allowed, the **Sørlandet** visited the Chicago World's Fair in 1933. Captured by the Germans in 1940 and turned into a floating prison for army deserters, she sank in northern Norway's Kirkenes harbor after being struck by a Russian bomb. A complete postwar refit brought her back into service in 1948; she was the last pure sailing ship used for training until 1960, when a diesel engine was added. Today, the 186-foot-long ship uses 10,165 square feet of polyester fabric sails and carries a complement of nineteen crew and seventy young trainees.*

THE
PARADE

How It All Began

"This is what we would do in any national emergency," said a port safety officer in the U.S. Coast Guard. He was talking about the preparations for Liberty Weekend, as tens of thousands of vessels aimed toward New York Harbor. In fact, "crisis management" was a phrase heard frequently in the nervous weeks before the largest nautical gathering in history.

Tongue in cheek, but with more than a little wariness, officials involved in the multitude of activities spoke of the coming "invasion". Millions of Americans were expected to pour into the Greater New York area. The city's public services, strained any normal business day to the crumbling point, were considered particularly vulnerable to stress. Where would disaster strike?

At every level of public and private participation in the celebration, the word went out: be prepared for the worst.

Something like $5.7 million in overtime pay was set aside for New York's policemen and city workers. To coordinate security for the weekend, more than 50 military, law-enforcement, emergency and other agencies met together 175 times. Three times the normal number of police officers were scheduled for duty in the city on July 4, backed up by park rangers, Federal customs agents, with their bomb-sensitive canines, and frogmen.

Not all preparations were quite so grim, expensive or comprehensive, but the statistics still startled. It was a nice idea to plant red, white and blue petunias down along the harborfront in Battery Park. But to make any visual impact in that sweeping exposure, it proved necessary to plant 45,000 of the flowers. A fifty-block area of downtown Manhattan, including the five acres of the World

Trade Center, was designated the Harbor Festival area. There, licenses were granted to about 500 concessions, many offering unusual ethnic and "designer" foods.

Yet for all the concrete preparations, the shape of the actual birthday celebration remained hazily indistinct beforehand. Would 13,000,000 people actually throng to the banks of the Hudson, as some predicted? Or would most people stay home, joining a projected 100,000,000 television viewers worldwide, rather than brave the crowds, five-borough hospitality, striking cab drivers, depressing subways and other mild horrors mentioned daily with puckish glee on the local TV news programs? Would there be violence, despite all the precautions? Would the whole thing be a bust?

While commentators, organizers and the general public pondered and made uneasy wisecracks, the countdown was inexorable. It was clear that at least 40,000 craft, from kayaks to the world's largest aircraft carrier, would be on hand by July 4. Participants with a long memory or a quick sense of history were fond of pointing out that D-Day, the invasion of Europe in World War II, had involved only 7,500 vessels. And D-Day has become a figure of speech for a mammoth, world-altering event. At least 25,000 crew members would be coming to the town and its pleasure spots. These projections of man and machine had the Coast Guard raising its complement of 12 boats stationed at Governors Island to about 340, including civilian auxiliaries. The Red Cross prepared 70 assistance centers, complete with computer hook-ups.

If these figures began to lose precision of meaning, the financial news in the days of anticipation before Liberty Weekend became even more difficult to grasp, in any useful way. The campaign to raise $265 million for the restoration of the Statue of Liberty and Ellis Island had surpassed its goal by $12 million. Meanwhile, it was estimated that entertainment planned by a Hollywood producer would cost $30 million, although advertising and other revenues were supposed to cover the costs and perhaps turn a profit. Whatever was going to happen, it was going to be big. Bigger than, well . . . No one was quite sure. But big.

Obviously, in the age of television, coverage of the event (and coverage of the coverage) would require strategies and investment commensurate with the event itself, and so it proved. In what one network news vice-president described as "the most complicated piece of logistics any of us can remember", one network set up 113 camera locations, 44 microwave dishes, 10 remote trucks and 7 cranes for camera and microwave transmissions. Another network reported that its coverage of the three-day event had required eight months of intensive work. During the weekend, the various local, national and international broadcasters would use something like 1,200 audio and video frequencies, a scarcely imaginable barrage of invisible waves piercing the atmosphere from the mouth of the Hudson.

Even the humble things of life loomed large in foresight. The police would need 36.8 miles of tape and twine. It would be necessary to set out 560 public toilets for the Harbor Festival. Because boats could be expected to capsize, hospitals ordered up extra stocks of Mylar blankets; administrators ordered increased supplies of insulin, just in case visiting diabetics ran out or lost their own.

All in all, expectation vied with fear, experience with the unpredictable, as hundreds of thousands of Americans worked to plan a celebration that, it was hoped, could be a tribute to liberty, not license. Could the weekend be a triumph of efficiency, yet seem a spontaneous outpouring of joy and communal feeling? Could the "invasion" come off without a hitch, and the invaders join together in the century's most memorable national picnic and rededication to shared ideals?

Let the following pages bear witness . . .

Thirty-six low-slung barges, known as "boyars", were transported from Amsterdam Harbor on a cargo ship. Many of these craft, when docked along Dutch canals, are homes for families, many of whom participated in Liberty Weekend.

*Reproductions of beloved, historically significant and simply notorious old sailing ships brought delighted applause during the day. The **Bounty,** at left, fired her cannon frequently, as if bent on capturing New York. The **Lady Barbara**, right, was in her own way no less swashbuckling a performer.*

The Day Itself

In the event, the Lady's birthday turned out to be a mammoth downhome reunion, a gathering of the American family from coast to coast. Spectacle awed, superlatives were put to the test, but the day in New York harbor felt pretty much like a covered-dish supper on the ground in Georgia or a cookout in the Midwestern plains. It was an occasion of gentle good times and high humor.

Weather helped, and in less secular times would have been considered sure proof of divine favor. The dank metropolitan air had been swept clean by night winds, the blue sky was lacquer-bright, and the day's breezes were subtle, insistent and welcome, gusting from 10 to 20 knots. Humidity, summer scourge of cities along the Atlantic, fell back to Edenic level. The discomfort index collapsed. The unusually low mean temperature was 66 degrees.

Whether in bikini or lightweight sports outfits, people were in more than fine spirits, as the day wound languidly through the Parade of Sail and later events. The consensus was clear: this was one of the great days in the American story. There was a moving blend of casual enjoyment—a holiday, after all—and respect for the traditions honored by that holiday. It was at once a celebration of summer joys and a tribute to the success of two centuries of national challenge.

Appropriately, the official festivities began at 8 A.M. with President Reagan boarding the battleship *Iowa* for her stately progress southward down the Hudson from Manhattan's mid-fifties. The mighty war engine, 887 feet long and 108 feet tall, fired salutes toward the 32 craft anchored in the

International Naval Review fleet. Noise was palpable, but not ominous. It was the boom of power held in reserve, or so it seemed to most observers. (Actually, in saluting, the *Iowa* used its 5-inch guns only, not its 16-inch heavy artillery, which in New York would probably have shattered windows and other exposed glass.) Answering 21-gun salutes came from such foreign vessels as Britain's aircraft carrier *Ark Royal*, France's helicopter carrier *Jeanne D'Arc*, Japan's destroyer *Nagatsuki*, West Germany's frigate *Braunschweig*, and Canada's destroyer *Iroquois*. The sounds of war, the vessels of opposition, were united in hoopla, and the point was made to begin the day: much of the world shared in the country's pride and excitement.

As the *Iowa* dropped anchor off Staten Island, the tens of thousands of pleasure craft that had spent the night in berths on the Hudson, the East River and Long Island Sound gathered in remarkably orderly fashion for the day's highlight, the Parade of Sail, in which the 235 Tall Ships and smaller sailing vessels would appear. Coast Guard personnel and auxiliary civilians sped to and fro, marshaling the myriad boats in a kind of nautical receiving line. The idea was to leave a 440-foot wide pathway from the Verrazano Bridge up to the George Washington Bridge.

At about 10:30, the *Eagle* materialized downstream from the crowd, veiled in mists dispersed by 100-foot tall water plumes pumped from two handmaiden fireboats. Shouts and cheers spattered across the waters, as aerobatic jet teams from France, Britain and the U.S. shrieked overhead. The day settled into a long, slow, fulfilling panoply of sail.

Time stopped, and no one seemed to mind. For some, there were ships that had special meaning, and spectators hailed their favorites. Some ships gained attention because of unusual markings, or a brilliantly covered sail, or a particularly photogenic crew. It is fair to report that the men of the *Amerigo Vespucci* placed first in the hearts of women in attendance. The grandest of the school ships provoked oohs and aahs, quite literally. Many ships had furled some sail, but were no less warmly applauded as they nosed northward. The restored *Elissa* was a special crowd favorite, perhaps because her delicate beauty belied her long, checkered history—or because her arrival was touching evidence that famous Texas spunk was still alive and optimistic, despite economic distress in the oil market. The *Christian Radich* was instantly recognized; as the first Tall Ship to make port earlier in the week, she had reaped reams of publicity from a city eager for the curtain to go up.

According to the arcane and insufficient science of crowd estimation, there were about a million and a half people lining the shores of the area. Another 10,000 stood along pedestrian walkways of the George Washington Bridge. Untold hundreds of thousands found good vantage points in apartments, restaurants and office buildings on both sides of the Hudson. There were brunches, lunches and other social gatherings, with the ships upon the glistening river as focus. There were also frolic and drink upon the water, but the mood did not turn ugly throughout the long bright day. Even more surprising, there were very few accidents and no serious unjuries reported.

After reaching the bridge upstream, each of the sailing ships turned around and came back to her assigned berth along the Hudson or in Brooklyn. By late afternoon, the unique parade had ended, and millions of people began to move into position for the evening's fireworks. Some went ashore for food and drink at the Harbor Festival, where various kinds of dancing, craft displays and other affirmations of ethnic identity attracted perhaps 2 million people. Other people stayed where they were, happy to have discovered the perfect anchorage or rooftop perspective.

At 9:30 P.M., while there was still some slight hint of azure in the summer heavens, the great roar and visual splash of fireworks began. From 41 barges moored around the southern tip of Manhattan from the Brooklyn Bridge on the East River to the World Trade Center, a barrage began that would send up 40,000 skyrockets within less than half an hour. Ten tons of explosives bathed the Statue of Liberty and the sprawling assemblage gathered in her honor with radiant fires of red, white, green, yellow, blue and orange. Shells burst in fantastic geometrics and arching flowers that made every man and woman there a delighted child.

At last, the happy day dwindled back to post-midnight realities. The city was still negotiable—not all of the expected millions came—but highways began to clog, tempers to flare, and the subways were overmatched by the crowds. Already, as the concrete streets gave back some of the day's warmth, the weather was changing; the following day would soar to the nineties, sticky with returned humidity. The party had crested.

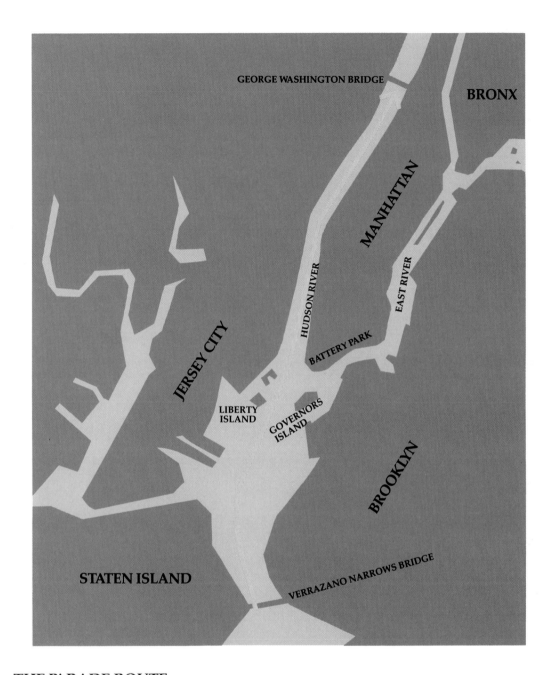

THE PARADE ROUTE

Led by the Coast Guard's *Eagle*, the great Parade of Sail started from the Verrazano
Bridge at 10 A.M. The Parade began to pass the Battery at noon and continued
until approximately 4 P.M., sailing up the Hudson to the George Washington Bridge
and back down the river to assigned berths and anchorages on both shores of the
Hudson and in Brooklyn.

XIV

*The glitzy conclave of private luxury yachts included the **Highlander**, owned by colorful publisher and balloonist Malcolm Forbes, Jr.*

Of the many souvenirs available in all price ranges, the most popular of all was a simple foam Liberty crown, an egalitarian and humorous memento that for many captured the day's spirit of relaxed fun.

*An eye-catching beauty popular with the July 4 crowd, the **Jessica** is a private yacht built three years ago for a rumored cost of approximately $8 million. Her sails are hoisted electrically and have pulled her through the water at more than 14 knots. A crew of twelve mans this lovely schooner and attends to the needs and whims of the fortunate eight guests aboard.*

*Aptly named, the tiny **Resolute** somehow managed to balance a huge and fluttering Old Glory all the way upstream and back.*

The contrasting color of the **Shamrock V**'s *sail, an emerald green rarely seen during the celebration, gladdened the heart of many an Irish-American there—presumably including one Ronald Reagan.*

No prizes were given for unusual entries in the Parade, but imaginative participants went all out anyway. The weird sphere, the kayak and the brightly colored junk were among the most playful attendants of the noble Tall Ships.

The **Ark Royal,** *newest aircraft carrier in the British fleet, is fifth in the nation's history to bear the name, including the 16th-century warship purchased by the Crown from Sir Walter Raleigh and the first ship built specifically as an aircraft carrier. Today's* **Ark Royal,** *680 feet long, is an antisubmarine carrier designed to serve as a command ship and to carry Britain's vertical-takeoff-and-landing Sea Harrier fighter planes. When she arrived to participate in the Naval Review of OpSail '86, she was escorted by the frigates* **Cleopatra** *and the* **Sirius.**

A stolid sentinel "showing the flag" at the start of the Parade, the 1,050-foot aircraft carrier **John F. Kennedy** was the day's vantage point for President and Mrs. Reagan and their guests.

*The **Deed of Gift** to the Statue of Liberty symbolically presented again by President Mitterrand to President Reagan on Governors Island on July 4, 1986. The Deed was displayed as part of Operation Sail's "Documents of Liberty" exhibition at Federal Hall; which also included the **Magna Carta** and Emma Lazarus' original manuscript of her poem, "The New Colossus".*

Perhaps, indeed, these vessels embody our conception of liberty itself, to have before one no impediments, only open spaces to chart one's own course, to take the adventure as it comes, to be free as the wind, as free as the tall ships themselves.

—President Ronald Reagan
July 4, 1986

JULY 4, 1986